Excel 365
LOOKUP Functions

EASY EXCEL 365 ESSENTIALS - BOOK 6

M.L. HUMPHREY

CONTENTS

Introduction

This book is part of the *Easy Excel 365 Essentials* series of titles. These are targeted titles that are excerpted from the main *Excel 365 Essentials* series and are focused on one specific topic.

If you want a more general introduction to Excel, then you should check out the *Excel 365 Essentials* titles instead. In this case, *102 Useful Excel 365 Functions* which covers the various LOOKUP functions as well as a number of other functions.

But if all you want is a book that covers this specific topic, then let's continue with a discussion of how to use VLOOKUP, HLOOKUP, and the new and incredibly useful XLOOKUP.

The **XLOOKUP, VLOOKUP,** and **HLOOKUP** Functions

I have high hopes for XLOOKUP, but this is the first time I've ever tried to use it, so let's see if it lives up to my imagined hype. (Hint: It does!) Before we get there, though, let's talk about VLOOKUP and HLOOKUP so you can put XLOOKUP into context.

VLOOKUP and HLOOKUP work in the same general way. They look in a range of values (either vertical for VLOOKUP or horizontal for HLOOKUP) and then when they find an exact match, or the closest match if that's the choice you've made, they return that value or a value in a related range of values.

Sounds complex, so let's go back to the example we just used with IF and IFS and use VLOOKUP instead to show you what I'm talking about.

	A	B	C	D
1	Spend X or More	Get Percent Discount		
2	$0.00	0%		
3	$25.00	5%		
4	$75.00	10%		
5	$150.00	20%		
6	$250.00	25%		
7				
8	Customer Spend	Discount Percent	Customer Final Cost	VLOOKUP Formula for Column B
9	$12.50	0%	$12.50	=VLOOKUP(A9,$A$1:$B$6,2,TRUE)
10	$25.00	5%	$23.75	=VLOOKUP(A10,$A$1:$B$6,2,TRUE)
11	$40.00	5%	$38.00	=VLOOKUP(A11,$A$1:$B$6,2,TRUE)
12	$75.00	10%	$67.50	=VLOOKUP(A12,$A$1:$B$6,2,TRUE)
13	$100.00	10%	$90.00	=VLOOKUP(A13,$A$1:$B$6,2,TRUE)
14	$150.00	20%	$120.00	=VLOOKUP(A14,$A$1:$B$6,2,TRUE)
15	$200.00	20%	$160.00	=VLOOKUP(A15,$A$1:$B$6,2,TRUE)
16	$250.00	25%	$187.50	=VLOOKUP(A16,$A$1:$B$6,2,TRUE)

The discount table is structured *almost* perfectly for use with VLOOKUP. What it was missing is that new first row in the table that says $0 and 0%. Without that first row the $12.50 customer purchase generates an error message.

The reason this discount table is structured so well for use with VLOOKUP is because the entries are in order and the amount spent column is the first column in the range.

I tend to hate working with VLOOKUP (although I've come around some) because the places where I want to use it do not include sorted data. Or I want to look a value up in Column E and return a value in Column C and that is not possible with VLOOKUP. So before I can ever use it I have to sort and rearrange my data, which is annoying.

But that's what you have to do.

So. Let's walk through the formula I wrote here and talk about the different components.

=VLOOKUP(A9,$A$1:$B$6,2,TRUE)

The first input, lookup_value, is the value you want to look up in your data range. In this case that's the amount that particular customer spent, which in Row 9 is in Cell A9.

The next input is your data table which Excel calls your table array. The first column of this range of cells MUST be the column that contains the values you want to compare to. So if I had an extra column to the left of the cutoffs for each discount, I'd have to leave that out of the table array. Excel with VLOOKUP will always look in the first column that you give for the table array. Always.

The table array you provide also has to include the column that contains the value you want to return. Here I'm asking Excel to take the amount the customer spent, compare it to my discount thresholds (Column A), and then return the discount percent (Column B). So the table array I provide has to include both of those columns. The discount thresholds and the discount percent.

You could technically have a table array that was one column. If I wanted to instead return the threshold amount that applied for that customer spend level, I could write a VLOOKUP function that only had one column for the table array.

But here we have two.

The next input, col_index, is the column number within the table array that contains the value you want to return. To get this number, look at the range you provided Excel in the last input, and then count which column from the start contains the value you want to return. In this instance it's very simple. I have two columns and the value I want back is the one from the second column so I use 2 for that.

The final input, range_lookup, is a TRUE/FALSE value. It's optional, because it will have a value of TRUE by default.

TRUE means look for the closest match. FALSE means look for an exact match. If you use TRUE, your data must be sorted.

In this case, we want the closest match not an exact match, because anything between $25 and $74.99 earns a discount of 5%. It doesn't have to be only $25 or only $75 to earn a discount which is what using an exact match would do.

So I used TRUE. I could have also left it blank and it would have generated the same result. Like this:

$$=VLOOKUP(A9,\$A\$1:\$B\$6,2)$$

(I include it because that makes me think through what I'm doing and make a conscious decision about it.)

It's important to understand what Excel considers the closest match. As I understand it, VLOOKUP (and HLOOKUP) starts with the first value in the first column (or row) of the range and compares that to your value.

If your value is greater than the first value, it keeps going until it finds a value that is greater than the one you're looking up. At that point, it drops back to the last value you passed. So for $12.50 it drops back to the value of $0 in our table. For $40 it drops back to $25.

For $74.99 it would still drop back to $40 even though it's only 1 cent from $75. So "closest" is a bit of a misnomer. It's actually "closest without going over".

But when your data is out of order, it really does weird things. I honestly can't figure out the pattern it follows.

Here I've taken our data table and messed with the order of the values in the table:

	A	B	C	D
1	Spend X or More	Get Percent Discount		
2	$150.00	20%		THESE RESULTS ARE WRONG
3	$0.00	0%		
4	$250.00	25%		
5	$25.00	5%		
6	$75.00	10%		
7				
8	Customer Spend	Discount Percent	Customer Final Cost	VLOOKUP Formula for Column B
9	$12.50	0%	$12.50	=VLOOKUP(A9,$A$1:$B$6,2,TRUE)
10	$25.00	5%	$23.75	=VLOOKUP(A10,$A$1:$B$6,2,TRUE)
11	$40.00	5%	$38.00	=VLOOKUP(A11,$A$1:$B$6,2,TRUE)
12	$75.00	10%	$67.50	=VLOOKUP(A12,$A$1:$B$6,2,TRUE)
13	$100.00	10%	$90.00	=VLOOKUP(A13,$A$1:$B$6,2,TRUE)
14	$150.00	10%	$135.00	=VLOOKUP(A14,$A$1:$B$6,2,TRUE)
15	$200.00	10%	$180.00	=VLOOKUP(A15,$A$1:$B$6,2,TRUE)
16	$250.00	10%	$225.00	=VLOOKUP(A16,$A$1:$B$6,2,TRUE)

Nothing else has changed. The formulas are the same. The discount levels are the same. The only change I made was making it so that the discount levels are not in ascending order. And you can see that Excel now pulls in wrong values. Everything from $75 and up returns a discount of 10%, even the rows that are an exact match like $250. And trying to apply logic from either the bottom or the top doesn't work.

Anyway. Be careful on those closest matches that you really understand what it's returning and that your data is sorted.

(Yes, I am going to say that a dozen times because it is so, so important. Sort your data when working with VLOOKUP and HLOOKUP unless you use exact matches.)

Okay. In the example above, the lookup column and the result column were right next to each other, but that doesn't have to be the case. I've had situations where the column I wanted a result from was the fifth, or sixth, or seventh. That is fine to do.

For example, I have an advertising tracker that uses VLOOKUP to bring in the book identifier number, author name, and series name from my Title Master Listing worksheet when I enter a title in Column E. Here's what those formulas look like for a couple of rows of that worksheet:

	F	G	H
1	ASIN	Author	Series
5222	=VLOOKUP(E5222,'Title Master Listing'!A:D,2,FALSE)	=VLOOKUP(E5222,'Title Master Listing'!A:D,3,FALSE)	=VLOOKUP(E5222,'Title Master Listing'!A:D,4,FALSE)
5223	=VLOOKUP(E5223,'Title Master Listing'!A:D,2,FALSE)	=VLOOKUP(E5223,'Title Master Listing'!A:D,3,FALSE)	=VLOOKUP(E5223,'Title Master Listing'!A:D,4,FALSE)
5224	=VLOOKUP(E5224,'Title Master Listing'!A:D,2,FALSE)	=VLOOKUP(E5224,'Title Master Listing'!A:D,3,FALSE)	=VLOOKUP(E5224,'Title Master Listing'!A:D,4,FALSE)

The formulas for Row 5222 are:

$$=VLOOKUP(E5222,'Title\ Master\ Listing'!A:D,\mathbf{2},FALSE)$$

$$=VLOOKUP(E5222,'Title\ Master\ Listing'!A:D,\mathbf{3},FALSE)$$

$$=VLOOKUP(E5222,'Title\ Master\ Listing'!A:D,\mathbf{4},FALSE)$$

I have bolded in those formulas above the only difference that exists between them, which is which column to pull a result from.

For each one, it looks at the title in Column E, and the source table it looks in is stored in Columns A through D of the Title Master Listing worksheet. Column A is Title. Column B is Identifier (ASIN). Column C is Author. Column D is Series.

So for ASIN I pull from the second column, for Author I pull from the third column, and for Series I pull from the fourth.

Note here that the last input is FALSE because I only want exact matches. If there isn't an exact match I'll get an error message that lets me know I need to update the table with information for that new title. That also means that my title master listing does not have to be sorted alphabetically, which is nice because that lets me just add new titles to the bottom of the list.

* * *

One more thing to emphasize. Both examples I just showed you have Column A as the lookup column, but that does not have to be the case.

You could have your lookup value in Column E. Or Column AEZ, for that matter. The key with VLOOKUP is that the first column *in the provided range* is the lookup column. So if it's Column E or Column AEZ then everything else has to be to the right of that column.

* * *

HLOOKUP is just like VLOOKUP except it looks for values across the first row in a range and then returns a value from that same column in the row that you specify. Here's an example:

	A	B	C	D	E	F	G	H	I
1			Vendor						
2		Amazon	Kobo	Nook	Google				
3	January	833	171	175	185		Nook		Formula
4	February	998	138	167	230		January	175	=HLOOKUP($G$3,$A$2:$E$8,2,FALSE)
5	March	1,102	221	200	142		February	167	=HLOOKUP($G$3,$A$2:$E$8,3,FALSE)
6	April	1,246	143	171	168				
7	May	941	186	181	250				
8	June	893	238	226	153				

I structured this example so that the data table starts in Row 2 instead of Row 1 so you can see that just like with VLOOKUP the data range doesn't have to be the first row (or column in the case of VLOOKUP).

What we have here is a data table in Columns A through E. Across Row 2, I've listed various vendors that sell my books. In Column A I have different months. And then the table shows (completely made-up) values for units sold in each month at those stores.

I've used HLOOKUP to look for the number of units sold in the Nook store in January and February. Here's the January formula:

$$=HLOOKUP(\$G\$3,\$A\$2:\$E\$8,2,FALSE)$$

Cell G3 contains the store name, Nook, that we want to look up. I've merged and centered that value across Columns G and H, but the value to Excel is stored in G3.

Next is our table range. That's A2 through E8. The first row of the table range needs to be the one that Excel will use to look up the value. In this case, Row 2. We leave out the label in Row 1, Vendor.

After that, for January, it's the second row in the range we provided Excel. It is not Row 2, it is the second row in the range A2:E8.

And then finally, I need an exact match, so I use FALSE. This means my data does not have to be sorted alphabetically left to right.

* * *

Okay. On to XLOOKUP which solves all the issues I have with using VLOOKUP and HLOOKUP. (Before we do this, part of the reason I still covered VLOOKUP in such detail is because people who have used it for years are still going to continue to use it, so you need to understand what they're doing when they do so.)

Let's play with XLOOKUP now and see how they've made our lives easier. I want to work with a new data table that has issues that always trip me up with VLOOKUP and HLOOKUP, so let's put something together that has unsorted values and has what we want to return to the left of what we want to look up.

Here we go, some random book information:

	A	B	C	D	E	F	G
1	Author Name	Title	Related Series	Wordcount	Hours to Write	Genre	
2	Author A	Title A	Series A	26,527	26.5	Non-Fiction	
3	Author B	Title B	Series B	46,204	54.25	Spec Fiction	
4	Author A	Title C	Series C	7,893	6	Non-Fiction	
5	Author B		Series B	6,079	4	Spec Fiction	
6	Author A	Title E	Series C	4,997	4	Non-Fiction	
7	Author A	Title F	Series C	7,976	4.25	Non-Fiction	
8	Author A	Title G	Series C	57,900	23	Non-Fiction	
9	Author A	Title H	Series A	8,284	5.75	Non-Fiction	
10							
11	Lookup Value		For	Result	Formula		
12	Title C		Author	Author A	=XLOOKUP(A12,B2:B9,A2:A9,"Title Not Found",0,1)		
13	Title C		Genre	Non-Fiction	=XLOOKUP(A13,B2:B9,F2:F9,"Title Not Found",0,1)		
14	Title D		Author	Title Not Found	=XLOOKUP(A14,B2:B9,A2:A9,"Title Not Found",0,1)		
15	Title D		Genre	Title Not Found	=XLOOKUP(A15,B2:B9,F2:F9,"Title Not Found",0,1)		

I have put the column with the unique values, Title, second. You can see that the author name (in Column A) and series name (in Column C) repeat, but title values in this data table are unique.

And that's probably something to emphasize here for all of these functions. They're built to retrieve information related to unique entries. The examples Excel uses are things like employee data with an employee ID number. You could likewise use it for customer information where there's a customer ID. Or, as we've done, with numeric values in a discount table.

What you don't want to ever do is try to use it on a table of information where the value you're searching for repeats because the function can only pull one result for you. You'll pull *a* result but not *the* result because there is not a single result to pull.

Like in this table. If I pull title for Author A, there are six potential results. Excel can only return one of those.

So.

Whatever values you are going to look up, in this case, title, need to be unique values in your data table. That doesn't mean you have to have exact matches. We didn't in our discount table, right? But it does mean that for $25 in spend, there should only be one discount to pull.

Okay, putting that digression aside. What do we have here?

Column A is author name, Column B is title, Column C is series name, Column D is wordcount, Column E is hours to write, and Column F is genre. With this particular set of data, the only column I would feel comfortable using as my lookup column is Column B, title. All other columns in this data table could have duplicate values.

That data is in Rows 1 through 9. Starting in Row 11 I have the results of some XLOOKUP formulas applied to that table. Rows 12 and 13 looked for Title C and returned the Author and Genre, respectively. Rows 14 and 15 tried to do the same for Title D, but there is no Title D in the table.

Let's look at the formula used in Row 12:

$$=XLOOKUP(A12,B2:B9,A2:A9,"Title Not Found",0,1)$$

It starts the exact same as VLOOKUP and HLOOKUP. What value do we want to look up? In this case, the answer to that is the value in Cell A12, "Title C".

Next, we need to tell Excel where to look. This is different. We are no longer providing a data table for this one. It's just the cells that contain the values we want to look at to see if we can find Title C. In this case that's Cells B2 through B9.

After that we provide a second cell range. That second cell range is where we want to pull the return value from. So, okay, you found my title for me, great, now go to this other range of cells and return the corresponding value for me.

In Row 12 that's returning the Author Name from Column A.

Because XLOOKUP doesn't use a data table like HLOOKUP and VLOOKUP did, you need to be sure that the cell range you provide for where to look and then what to return are the same size.

XLOOKUP also has some fun bells and whistles there at the end. It lets you specify what text to return if there isn't a result. In other words, if it can't find a match to the value in Cell A12. That's important, because I initially misinterpreted it and thought it meant if there wasn't a value to return for author (in this example). But I was wrong.

That text is what you display if XLOOKUP can't find the match to what you asked it to look for. Which means I expect it only matters when you use an exact match.

Those last two inputs tell Excel about the type of match to return and how to look for results.

Match mode is the first of those two. It has four potential choices, 0, -1, 1, and 2.

The default is an exact match. (Yay, unlike VLOOKUP and HLOOKUP.) You can either leave this field blank and just put a comma to move to the next input or you can provide a value of 0, like I did.

If there is no exact match AND you didn't tell it what text to return then it will return a result of #N/A.

The next choice is exact match, but if none is found return the next smallest value. Use a negative one (-1) for that.

Then you have exact match, but if none is found return the next largest value. (Exciting that you have this choice now.) Use a one (1) for that.

And finally you can use a two (2) for a wildcard-type match that uses the * and ? that we discussed with COUNTIFS.

After match mode you can specify a search mode.

The default for that is to start with the first item, so you can leave it blank if you want. Or you can use a one like I did in the example above.

A negative one (-1) will search from the last item.

A two (2) is what to use when the data is sorted in ascending order.

A negative two (-2) is what to use when the data is sorted in descending order.

So much more control! This is very exciting. I know you aren't feeling it the way I am, but it is.

Let's circle back to our earlier examples that used VLOOKUP and HLOOKUP and let's replace those with XLOOKUP.

Here's our first VLOOKUP discount table example, but with XLOOKUP instead:

	A	B	C	D
1	Spend X or More	Get Percent Discount		
2	$0.00	0%		
3	$25.00	5%		
4	$75.00	10%		
5	$150.00	20%		
6	$250.00	25%		
7				
8	Customer Spend	Discount Percent	Customer Final Cost	XLOOKUP Formula for Column B
9	$12.50	0%	$12.50	=XLOOKUP(A9,$A$2:$A$6,$B$2:$B$6,,-1,2)
10	$25.00	5%	$23.75	=XLOOKUP(A10,$A$2:$A$6,$B$2:$B$6,,-1,2)
11	$40.00	5%	$38.00	=XLOOKUP(A11,$A$2:$A$6,$B$2:$B$6,,-1,2)
12	$75.00	10%	$67.50	=XLOOKUP(A12,$A$2:$A$6,$B$2:$B$6,,-1,2)
13	$100.00	10%	$90.00	=XLOOKUP(A13,$A$2:$A$6,$B$2:$B$6,,-1,2)
14	$150.00	20%	$120.00	=XLOOKUP(A14,$A$2:$A$6,$B$2:$B$6,,-1,2)
15	$200.00	20%	$160.00	=XLOOKUP(A15,$A$2:$A$6,$B$2:$B$6,,-1,2)
16	$250.00	25%	$187.50	=XLOOKUP(A16,$A$2:$A$6,$B$2:$B$6,,-1,2)

The formula for the value in Cell A9 is now:

=XLOOKUP(A9,$A$2:$A$6,$B$2:$B$6,,-1,2)

That says, look for the value in Cell A9 in the range of cells between A2 and A6. Return the value in B2 through B6. Don't return text if there's no match. (That's the nothing between those commas there.)

And then I used -1 for the match mode, which drops down to the lower discount level when there's no exact match and a number is between two values. (So $40 goes to $25 not $75.)

And 2 for the search mode to say that my data table was sorted in ascending order.

And it works! Woohoo. I really like XLOOKUP. Thank you Excel folks.

Next. Let's look at the unsorted discount table that didn't work with VLOOKUP.

	A	B	C	D
1	Spend X or More	Get Percent Discount		
2	$150.00	20%		
3	$0.00	0%		
4	$250.00	25%		
5	$25.00	5%		
6	$75.00	10%		
7				
8	Customer Spend	Discount Percent	Customer Final Cost	XLOOKUP Formula for Column B
9	$12.50	0%	$12.50	=XLOOKUP(A9,$A$2:$A$6,$B$2:$B$6,,-1,1)
10	$25.00	5%	$23.75	=XLOOKUP(A10,$A$2:$A$6,$B$2:$B$6,,-1,1)
11	$40.00	5%	$38.00	=XLOOKUP(A11,$A$2:$A$6,$B$2:$B$6,,-1,1)
12	$75.00	10%	$67.50	=XLOOKUP(A12,$A$2:$A$6,$B$2:$B$6,,-1,1)
13	$100.00	10%	$90.00	=XLOOKUP(A13,$A$2:$A$6,$B$2:$B$6,,-1,1)
14	$150.00	20%	$120.00	=XLOOKUP(A14,$A$2:$A$6,$B$2:$B$6,,-1,1)
15	$200.00	20%	$160.00	=XLOOKUP(A15,$A$2:$A$6,$B$2:$B$6,,-1,1)
16	$250.00	25%	$187.50	=XLOOKUP(A16,$A$2:$A$6,$B$2:$B$6,,-1,1)

And there it is. It works! (I may send a marriage proposal to whoever did the work on XLOOKUP. I'm serious. Not in a creepy way, but in a "thank you for removing the things that create so many user errors when people try to use VLOOKUP." This is one of those improvements that someone made to a long-running software program that has huge benefits for users which are quite frankly somewhat rare after a certain stage. But the COUNTIFS, SUMIFS, etc. changes a few releases back and this one are spot on, absolutely worth having the latest edition of the software sort of changes. Give those people some bonuses.)

Okay, enough gushing.

Here's the formula for Cell A9:

=XLOOKUP(A9,$A$2:$A$6,$B$2:$B$6,,-1,1)

The beginning of the formula is the exact same as last time. What's different is the final input. I used 1 here instead of 2, because the data is not sorted. Excel, behind the scenes, sorted the values and then looked through for the proper discount percents.

And it worked!

One last example. Our HLOOKUP example. Because I need to show you that this can work horizontally, too.

	A	B	C	D	E	F	G	H	I
1				Vendor					
2		Amazon	Kobo	Nook	Google				
3	January	833	171	175	185		Nook		Formula
4	February	998	138	167	230		January	175	=XLOOKUP(G3,B2:E2,B3:E3,,0,1)
5	March	1,102	221	200	142		February	167	=XLOOKUP(G3,B2:E2,B4:E4,,0,1)
6	April	1,246	143	171	168				
7	May	941	186	181	250				
8	June	893	238	226	153				

Here we are. Same data table we used for HLOOKUP, but now we have this formula for February:

$$=XLOOKUP(G3,B2:E2,B4:E4,,0,1)$$

First input, same as any of the examples, is the value we want to look for, in this case Nook that's in Cell G3.

Second input, where to look, is a range of cells across a row this time instead of down a column. That's Cells B2 through E2.

Third input is where to pull a result from. This is also a range of cells across a row. And just like with our columns, the size of the cell range needs to match the range we provided for where to look. So that's Cells B4 through E4.

I don't need it to return text if there's no match so I left it blank, that's the next comma.

And then I said Exact Match (0) and search first to last (1).

Since exact match and search first to last are the defaults and I'm okay returning #N/A if there's no match, I could also write that as:

$$=XLOOKUP(G3,B2:E2,B3:E3)$$

You can leave off those optional inputs at the end if you want to go with the default.

Okay. So that was VLOOKUP, HLOOKUP, and XLOOKUP. I think it was important to teach you VLOOKUP because it was a very, very popular function for many, many years so if you're going to work with other people who have been using Excel for a while it is almost a certainty that they will use VLOOKUP if they're programming sorts.

Also, there's that backwards compatibility issue. XLOOKUP has only just been widely released so most users with on-premise versions of Excel or older worksheets will still be using VLOOKUP and HLOOKUP.

But for a new user, if you don't have to worry about playing well with others, just go straight to XLOOKUP. It does everything VLOOKUP and HLOOKUP can do, but better. Beautiful.

Okay. Stop here if you just wanted the basics. There are a few more things you can do with XLOOKUP that I want to cover, but they may also be more than an average user wants to know. So if you're that average user, no worries, carry on and move to the next chapter.

But if you want to keep going…Here we go.

XLOOKUP can actually return multiple results. Remember my example above where I have a tracking worksheet that takes my title and then looks up an identifier, author name, and series name? And how that required three separate VLOOKUP functions?

We can use XLOOKUP to return all three at once. The formula becomes:

=XLOOKUP(E5222,'Title Master Listing'!A:A,'Title Master Listing'!B:D)

That works as long as the columns where I want those values returned match the order of those values in my Title Master Listing worksheet.

So what did I change here to make it do that? How does this work?

The first input is unchanged. What cell has the lookup value? E5222

The second input is also unchanged. What range should we look for title in? Column A in the Title Master Listing worksheet.

It's the third one that pulls the multiple values. Instead of putting 'Title Master Listing'!B:B so that Excel pulls the result from one column, we now have 'Title Master Listing'!B:**D** which is Columns B, C, and D. So Excel pulls the values across all three of those columns as its result.

Pretty cool, huh?

Because Excel returns results across columns (or rows) when you do this, you need to be deliberate about doing so because you need to make sure that the order between the lookup table and where you're placing those results match. You may also occasionally run into a #SPILL! error if there aren't enough blank cells available to display all of the returned values.

Another weird thing that XLOOKUP can do is it can actually look up two values and return all of the results in between. Here's a simple data table with total units sold per month for a year. (Randomly generated data using RANDBETWEEN for each quarter.)

	A	B	C	D	E	F	G
1		Units Sold		Start	End	Total	Formula
2	January	1,253		January	March	4076	=SUM(XLOOKUP(D2,$A$2:$A$13,$B$2:$B$13):XLOOKUP(E2,$A$2:$A$13,$B$2:$B$13))
3	February	1,417		April	June	2744	=SUM(XLOOKUP(D3,$A$2:$A$13,$B$2:$B$13):XLOOKUP(E3,$A$2:$A$13,$B$2:$B$13))
4	March	1,406		July	September	2106	=SUM(XLOOKUP(D4,$A$2:$A$13,$B$2:$B$13):XLOOKUP(E4,$A$2:$A$13,$B$2:$B$13))
5	April	929		October	December	3142	=SUM(XLOOKUP(D5,$A$2:$A$13,$B$2:$B$13):XLOOKUP(E5,$A$2:$A$13,$B$2:$B$13))
6	May	850					
7	June	965					
8	July	736					
9	August	660					
10	September	710					
11	October	1,041					
12	November	942					
13	December	1,159					

Column A is the month. Column B is the units. In Columns D and E I have months that set each quarterly range. So quarter one is January to March, quarter two is April to June, etc.

Column F is the calculation. Column G shows the formula used in Column F.

Here is the formula for the first quarter:

=SUM(XLOOKUP(D2,$A$2:$A$13,$B$2:$B$13):XLOOKUP(E2,$A$2:$A$13,$B$2:$B$13))

That looks complex, but it's basically the SUM function wrapped around two XLOOKUP functions that are separated with a colon (:) which is used to join the two ends of a cell range.

Let's pull out the first XLOOKUP function in the formula:

XLOOKUP(D2,$A$2:$A$13,$B$2:$B$13)

That says, look up the value in Cell D2 (January) in the range A2 through A13 and return the corresponding value in the range B2 through B13.

But here's where it gets weird. Behind the scenes, because it's the SUM function and we use the colon to separate the two uses of the XLOOKUP function, what we actually get is the cell reference for that result. It returns B2 in this case.

Same happens for the other XLOOKUP function. It returns B4.

And what we end up with is

=SUM(B2:B4)

which in this case is 4,076 for that first quarter.

I just tested this with the AVERAGE, COUNT, MIN, MAX, and PRODUCT functions as well and it still worked for each of them. So basically you can use XLOOKUP with other Excel functions where XLOOKUP sets the cell range to use in the function.

I haven't thought through all the implications of that yet, but I'd think that's pretty powerful. The reason I put it here in the "know more" portion of the chapter is because it's very counterintuitive to me that it works that way. I wouldn't expect it to return a cell reference, I'd expect it to return the value from that cell, so it's a little twisty to me how it works. But it does. So there you have it.

One more twisty example and then we really are going to be done with XLOOKUP. Here you go:

	A	B	C	D	E	F	G	H
1		Vendor						
2		Amazon	Kobo	Nook	Google			
3	January	833	171	175	185			
4	February	998	138	167	230			
5	March	1,102	221	200	142			
6	April	1,246	143	171	168			
7	May	941	186	181	250			
8	June	893	238	226	153			
9								
10								
11	Vendor	January	March	May				
12	Amazon	833	1102	941				
13	Kobo	171	221	186				
14								
15	Formula in B12	=XLOOKUP(B$11,$A$3:$A$8,XLOOKUP($A12,$B$2:$E$2,$B$3:$E$8))						

What we have here is a data table in Cells A1 through E8. There are four vendors and six months of results. Starting in Row 11 I have another table that lists two of those vendors in Cells A12 and A13 and asks for values for those two vendors for three different months, January, March, and May. That table uses XLOOKUP to populate the values in the table.

The formula you can see in Row 15 is the same as the one used in Cell B12:

$$=XLOOKUP(B\$11,\$A\$3:\$A\$8,XLOOKUP(\$A12,\$B\$2:\$E\$2,\$B\$3:\$E\$8))$$

This is a nested XLOOKUP formula that pulls in values when you feed it both the month and the vendor to look for. And it does so even though the source table has vendor across the top and month down the side and the data table to populate has those reversed.

You may be asking how on earth does it do that? Because it certainly wasn't obvious to me trying to "read" the formula.

A trick to see what's happening at each step for a formula is to click on that cell and then go to the Formula Auditing section of the Formulas tab and click on Evaluate Formula. This opens a dialogue box that lets you go through the formula step-by-step.

It's not entirely obvious even then, but what it looks like it does is this:

It replaces B11 and A12 with their text values first.

$$=XLOOKUP('January',\$A\$3:\$A\$8,XLOOKUP('Amazon',\$B\$2:\$E\$2,\$B\$3:\$E\$8))$$

After that it collapses down XLOOKUP('Amazon',$B$2:$E$2,$B$3:$E$8) to its column range result, Column B. So you get this:

$$=XLOOKUP('January',\$A\$3:\$A\$8,\$B\$3:\$B\$8))$$

From there it works just like a normal XLOOKUP function.

I would not have guessed that would be the next step it takes, but it is. This is a powerful and relatively simple use of XLOOKUP that can potentially replace a lookup I've seen that combines the INDEX and MATCH functions, but I think it's going to be one of those tools that's only accessible to more advanced users or those whose minds naturally twist in the right direction.

This is one of those times when Excel's help text is very useful. I was able to create the example above by looking at what they did with a table of corporate results for four quarters and then adapting it to my table. Never be scared to copy someone else's work in Excel. (Or if you ever get into programming.) You have to figure out which part is which and how they all work together, but if you can do that it's a lot easier than trying to start from scratch a lot of times with the more complex uses of functions.

So if you really want to get into this, type XLOOKUP and your opening paren and then click on that XLOOKUP in the box below the cell and read that whole long help article and try to come up with new scenarios for each of their examples and then try them out to test your understanding.

Appendix A: Basic Terminology

These terms are defined in detail in *Excel 365 for Beginners*. This is just a quick overview in case it's needed.

Workbook

A workbook is what Excel likes to call an Excel file.

Worksheet

Excel defines a worksheet as the primary document you use in Excel to store and work with your data. A worksheet is organized into Columns and Rows that form Cells. A workbook can contain multiple worksheets.

Columns

Excel uses columns and rows to display information. Columns run across the top of the worksheet and, unless you've done something funky with your settings, are identified using letters of the alphabet.

The first column in a worksheet will always be Column A. And the number of columns in your worksheet will remain the same, regardless of how many columns you delete, add, or move around. Think of columns as location information that is actually separate from the data in the worksheet.

Rows

Rows run down the side of each worksheet and are numbered starting at 1 and up to a very high number. Row numbers are also locational information. The first row will always be numbered 1, the second row will always be numbered 2, and so on and so forth. There will also always be a fixed number of rows in each worksheet regardless of how many rows of data you delete, add, or move around.

Cells

Cells are where the row and column data comes together. Cells are identified using the letter for the column and the number for the row that intersect to form that cell. For example, Cell A1 is the cell that is in the first column and first row of the worksheet.

Click

If I tell you to click on something, that means to use your mouse (or trackpad) to move the cursor on the screen over to a specific location and left-click or right-click on the option. If you left-click, this selects the item. If you right-click, this generally displays a dropdown list of options to choose from. If I don't tell you which to do, left- or right-click, then left-click.

Left-click/Right-click

If you look at your mouse you generally have two flat buttons to press. One is on the left side, one is on the right. If I say left-click that means to press down on the button on the left. If I say right-click that means press down on the button on the right.

Select

If I tell you to "select" cells, that means to highlight them. You can either left-click and drag to select a range of cells or hold down the Ctrl key as you click on individual cells. To select an entire column, click on the letter for the column. To select an entire row, click on the number for the row.

Data

Data is the information you enter into your worksheet.

Data Table

I may also sometimes refer to a data table or table of data. This is just a combination of cells that contain data in them.

Arrow

If I tell you to arrow to somewhere or to arrow right, left, up, or down, this just means use the arrow keys to navigate to a new cell.

Cursor Functions

The cursor is what moves around when you move your mouse or use the trackpad. In Excel the cursor changes its appearance depending on what functions you can perform.

Tab

I am going to talk a lot about Tabs, which are the options you have to choose from at the top of the workspace. The default tab names are File, Home, Insert, Page Layout, Formulas, Data, Review, View, and Help. But there are certain times when additional tabs will appear, for example, when you create a pivot table or a chart.

(This should not be confused with the Tab key which can be used to move across cells.)

Dropdown Menus

A dropdown menu is a listing of available choices that you can see when you right-click in certain places such as the main workspace or on a worksheet name. You will also see them when you click on an arrow next to or below an option in the top menu.

Dialogue Boxes

Dialogue boxes are pop-up boxes that contain additional choices.

Scroll Bars

When you have more information than will show in a screen, dialogue box, or dropdown menu, you will see scroll bars on the right side or bottom that allow you to navigate to see the rest of the information.

Formula Bar

The formula bar is the long white bar at the top of the main workspace directly below the top menu options that lets you see the actual contents of a cell, not just the displayed value.

Cell Notation

Cells are referred to by their column and row position. So Cell A1 is the cell that's the intersection of the first column and first row in the worksheet.

When written in Excel you just use A1, you do not need to include the word cell. A colon (:) can be used to reference a range of cells. A comma (,) can be used to separate cell references.

When in doubt about how to define a cell range, click into a cell, type =, and then go and select the cells you want to reference. Excel will describe your selection in the formula bar using cell notation.

Paste Special Values

Paste Special Values is a way of pasting copied values that keeps the calculation results or the cell values but removes any formulas or formatting.

Task Pane

On occasion Excel will open a task pane, which is different from a dialogue box because it is part of the workspace. These will normally appear on the right-hand side in Excel for tasks such as working with pivot tables or charts or using the built-in Help function. (They often appear on the left-hand side in Word.)

They can be closed by clicking on the X in the top right corner.

About the Author

M.L. Humphrey is a former stockbroker with a degree in Economics from Stanford and an MBA from Wharton who has spent close to twenty years as a regulator and consultant in the financial services industry.

You can reach M.L. at mlhumphreywriter@gmail.com or at mlhumphrey.com.

* * *

If you want to learn more about Microsoft Excel, check out *Excel Tips and Tricks* or one of the main Excel 365 Essentials titles, *Excel 365 for Beginners*, *Intermediate Excel 365*, or *102 Useful Excel 365 Functions*.

Printed in Great Britain
by Amazon

16890852R00016